Adventures in Penmanship

by Aanoyah D Sarmah

BLUEROSE PUBLISHERS
India | U.K.

Copyright ©c Aanoyah D Sarmah 2024

All rights reserved by author. No part of this publication may be reproduced, stored in a retrieval system or transmitted in any form or by any means, electronic, mechanical, photocopying, recording or otherwise, without the prior permission of the author. Although every precaution has been taken to verify the accuracy of the information contained herein, the publisher assume no responsibility for any errors or omissions. No liability is assumed for damages that may result from the use of information contained within.

BlueRose Publishers takes no responsibility for any damages, losses, or liabilities that may arise from the use or misuse of the information, products, or services provided in this publication.

For permissions requests or inquiries regarding this publication, please contact:

BLUEROSE PUBLISHERS
www.BlueRoseONE.com
info@bluerosepublishers.com
+91 8882 898 898
+4407342408967

ISBN: 978-93-6452-722-4

Cover design: Tahira
Typesetting: Tanya Raj Upadhyay

First Edition: September 2024

DEDICATION

For my father, who taught me how to tackle anything life threw my way. His absence is a constant reminder of the incredible person he was. This one's for you, Ditu.

PREFACE

I've always had a knack for words. It felt like a lightbulb moment when I got the idea – why not turn those random internet quotes into poems? So, I dove in, headfirst into the world of rhyme and rhythm. It was a way to process the messy tangle of teenage emotions, the stuff too raw to say out loud. Writing became my secret language, a medium where I could be honest without any fear of judgment. I poured my heart out into these poems, using words as a lifeline to navigate the stormy seas of adolescence. It was a cathartic process, like finding a hidden room in the midst of chaos where I could be utterly myself. I've always believed that the most honest art comes from the deepest corners of the soul, and I hope these poems resonate with anyone who's ever felt lost or misunderstood. Maybe, just maybe, these words can offer a sense of companionship to those who feel like they're navigating life's challenges alone. Because in the end, sharing our vulnerabilities is what connects us all.

TABLE OF CONTENTS

THE SEVEN DEADLY SINS 1
The 7 Deadly Sins- Envy 1
The 7 Deadly Sins- Gluttony 3
The 7 Deadly Sins- Greed 5
The 7 Deadly Sins- Lust 7
The 7 Deadly Sins- Pride 8
The 7 Deadly Sins- Sloth 10
The 7 Deadly Sins- Wrath 12

THE SEVEN HEAVENLY VIRTUES 13
The 7 Heavenly Virtues- Charity 13
The 7 Heavenly Virtues- Chastity 15
The 7 Heavenly Virtues- Diligence 17
The 7 Heavenly Virtues- Gratitude 19
The 7 Heavenly Virtues- Humility 21
The 7 Heavenly Virtues- Patience 23
The 7 Heavenly Virtues- Temperance 25
A Letter To My Future Self Never Give Up Because Great Things Take Time 27
A Soul Unseen 29
Be Loud About The Things That Are Important To You 31
Beauty Is Dangerous, But Intelligence Is Lethal 32
Being A Hero Doesn't Mean You're Invincible. It Just Means That You're Brave Enough To Stand Up And Do What's Needed 33

Books	34
Childhood	36
Confusion	38
Do You Ever Miss The Old You?	39
Don't Adapt The Energy In The Room. Influence The Energy In The Room.	40
Don't Fashion Me Into A Maiden That Needs Saving From A Dragon For I Am The Dragon.	41
Don't Worry Mother, Your Daughter Is A Soldier	42
Everyone Says Follow Your Heart But If My Heart Is In A Trillion Pieces Which Piece Do I Follow?	44
Forever Writing A Story In My Head	45
Global Warming	46
Go On With What Your Heart Tells You, Or You Will Lose All.	47
Good Friends Don't Let You Do Stupid Things Alone	48
Her Life Changed When She Learned The Monsters Were Protecting Her	50
Hope	51
How Does It Feel Like? To Be A Man?	53
I Am Not Afraid Of Storms, For I Am Learning How To Sail My Ship	55
I Feel Small, But So Are Stars From A Distance	57
I Know I'm Young But My Mind Is Well Beyond My Years	58
I Still Repeat The Things You Said To Me In My Head	59
I Was Born To Tell Stories	60

I Write Because I Don't Know What I Think Until I Read What I Say. 61

I Wrote A Poem About It, And Then Threw It Away 62

If I Disappear... Will You Look For Me? 63

If You Could Read My Mind, You'd Know How Hard I Tried 64

I'm Gonna Say "I Got This," Even With Tears In My Eyes 66

I'm Not In This World To Live Up To Your Expectations And You're Not In This World To Live Up To Mine 67

Imagination 68

In The End, We Will Remember Not The Words Of Our Enemies, But The Silence Of Our Friends 70

In The End... We'll All Become Memories 71

Is It My Fault Though? 72

It's Not How Long You Live That Matters. It's What You Live For. 73

I've Lived A Thousand Lives And Loved A Thousand Loves. I've Walked On Distant Shores And Seen The End Of Time. Because I Read. 74

Just Because I Don't Show It. Doesn't Mean I Don't Feel It. 75

Life Is Only Precious Because It Ends 76

Lillies 77

May The Gods Have Mercy On My Enemies. Because I Won't. 78

Maybe... Maybe Forever Is A Word Meant For Memories, Not People 79

My Thoughts Were Destroying Me. I Tried Not To
Think, But The Silence Was A Killer Too 80

Never Regret Anything That Made You Smile... Even
If It's For A Short Period Of Time....................................81

Nothing Is More Tragic Than Loving Someone To
The Depths Of Your Soul Knowing They Cannot And
Will Not Ever Love You Back...82

Poetry Doesn't Have To Rhyme, It Has To Touch
Somewhere Your Hands Couldn't....................................84

Push Yourself Because No One Else Is Going To Do It
For You 85

Questions 86

Raise Your Words Not Your Voice...................................88

Real Queens Fix Each Other's Crown 90

She Isn't Fragile Like A Flower. She Is Fragile Like
A Bomb. 92

She Needed A Hero, So That's What She Became 93

She Never Cared For A Crown. She Preferred A
Sword..95

She Remembered Who She Was, And The Game
Changed 97

She Used To Be The Sweetest Girl... 99

She Wore Her Scars As Her Best Attire, A Stunning
Dress Made Of Hellfire. 100

Some People Survive Chaos, And That Is How They
Grow, I Thrive In Chaos Because That Is All I Know..102

Sometimes, Happy Memories Hurt The Most.............103

Speak The Truth, Even If Your Voice Shakes 104

Sun-Moon 105

The Beautiful Spring Came, And When Nature Resumes Her Loveliness, The Human Soul Is Apt To Revive Also. 107

The Darkest Nights Produce The Brightest Stars 108

The Language Of Dance 109

The Power Of Imagination Makes Us Infinite 110

The Scariest Moment Is Always Before You Start 111

The Scariest Monsters Are The Ones That Lurk Within Our Souls 112

The Sound Of Joy 113

The Truth Is... I Am Not Sorry... Why Should I Be Sorry For The Things You Did? 114

The Truth? We'll Never Have Today Again. 115

The Woods Are Lovely, Dark, And Deep, But I Have Promises To Keep, And Miles To Go Before I Sleep 116

The Word "Father" Rotted In My Mouth 117

The Wound Is The Place Where The Light Enters You 118

There Is Always A Way Out For Those Clever Enough To Find It 119

There Is Nothing Either Good, Or Bad, But The Thinking Makes It So 120

They Broke The Wrong Parts Of Me. They Broke My Wings And Forgot I Had Claws............................. 121

They Asked- Don't You Feel Lonely Living In Your Own World? I Whispered- Don't You Feel Powerless Living In Other People's Worlds? 122

They're Villains...But Why? 124

Thunderstorms 126

To Be A Star, You Must Burn 128

To Live Is The Rarest Thing In The World. Most
People Exist, That Is All 129

We Are All Born So Beautiful, The Greatest Tragedy
Is Being Convinced We Are Not 130

We Cannot Become What We Want By Remaining
What We Are 131

What Lies Behind Us And What Lies Before Us Are
Tiny Matters Compared To What Lies Within Us 132

What's A Queen Without Her King? Well,
Historically Speaking, More Powerful 133

When You Get Tired, Learn To Rest, Not To Quit 135

Who Needs A Prince When You're Already A Queen? .136

You Don't Understand. It's Not That I Can't Love.
It's That I'm Afraid Of It...137

You Have To Be Odd To Be Number One 138

You Know What The Weirdest Is For Me? I Don't
Cry When I Lose The People I Love Anymore... 139

You Must Forge Your Own Path For It To Mean
Anything...141

THE SEVEN DEADLY SINS

The 7 Deadly Sins- Envy

In the depths of our souls, a sin does reside,
Envy, the beast that cannot be denied.
Like poison, it seeps into our veins,
Filling our hearts with jealous pains.

With eyes full of envy, we look upon others,
Wishing we had what they possess, including their lovers.
Their success, their fame, their fortune so grand,
We crave what they have, unable to withstand.

Envious whispers poison our thoughts,
As we compare ourselves and all that we've brought.
Our self-worth diminishes, consumed by green,
As envy's grip tightens, a wicked scene.

It consumes us wholly, this insidious desire,
For what we don't have, fuels a burning fire.
We yearn for more, discontent with our own,
In this never-ending cycle, our souls are overthrown.

We covet their beauty, their talents, their grace,
Envy twists our minds, leaving no trace.
It festers within, staining our soul,
Until envy's bitter fruit takes its toll.

The 7 Deadly Sins- Gluttony

In a realm where darkness thrives,
There lies a sin that truly connives,
Gluttony, the insatiable thirst,
Feeds on desires, though it's accursed.

With a voracious appetite, it devours,
Both the meagre and the dainty flowers,
Indulging in excess, without any halt,
Gluttony consumes, leaving hearts to fault.

With each bite, it craves for more,
Taking pleasures to the very core,
Feasting recklessly with insidious glee,
Gluttony indulges, imprisoning the free.

It craves for food, to fill the void,
But the emptiness can never be destroyed,
Swallowing ambition, like a bottomless pit,
Gluttony suffocates dreams bit by bit.

Obscenely indulging in all of life's pleasures,
It smothers the soul, igniting no treasures,
For gluttony knows no satiation,
Only a never-ending need for sensation.

Through feasts of grandeur and endless cheer,
It chips away at virtue, fostering fear,
As gluttony grows, consuming the weak,
Desire itself becomes what's bleak.

But let us remember, amidst this plight,
That gluttony's hold can be banished by light,
With self-control, we can seize the day,
And resist the cravings that lead us astray.

The 7 Deadly Sins- Greed

In the realm of sins, there lies Greed,
A haunting hunger, a ravenous need.
It grasps our souls with a wicked hand,
And leads us astray in a barren land.

Oh Greed, you temptress, your lure is strong,
Like a siren's song, seductive and wrong.
You whisper sweetly in the depths of our minds,
Fanning the flames of desires that bind.

For riches and fortunes, we yearn and we chase,
Counting our worth by the coins we embrace.
But in this pursuit, we lose our way,
Blinded by greed, we lose our say.

We crave more than plenty, more than our share,
Hoarding possessions without a care.
Our hunger devours us, an insatiable beast,
Leaving behind a void, a soul deceased.

Greed, with your claws, you tear us apart,
Stealing compassion, a poison to our heart.
We trample on others to reach the top,
Ignoring empathy as we greedily swap.

You corrupt our spirits, and stain our souls,
Turning them black just as coal, taking their tolls.
For in the grip of greed, we lose our grace,
And tarnish our humanity in our chase.

The 7 Deadly Sins- Lust

In a world of desires, where passions ignite,
Lust whispers its call, in the moon's gentle light.
An insatiable hunger that consumes the soul,
Magnetic attraction, it takes full control.

In the depths of desire, where yearning resides,
Lust tempts us to venture through uncharted tides.
With seductive gaze, it unveils its disguise,
Obeying its commands, our senses surmise.

With a glance, a touch, it ignites a flame,
Burning inside us, we can't help but acclaim.
Drowning in fantasies, we find no escape,
As Lust's spell entraps us, like an endless tape.

It takes many forms, this alluring sin,
A craving for pleasure, consumed from within.
Inflamed and corrupted, it blinds us with desire,
Leaving reason and morals to smoulder in its fire.

From stolen glances to forbidden embraces,
In pursuit of forbidden, we venture through puzzling mazes.
It tempts the pious, the innocent, and weak,
Its allure so consuming, that's the power we seek.

The 7 Deadly Sins- Pride

In the realm of sins, there lies one so wide,
A vice known as pride that swells with no stride.
Its roots deep-seated within the human heart,
Inflating the ego, tearing bonds apart.

Pride, a false prism that distorts the light,
Blinding one's vision with its dazzling might.
It whispers sweet praises, stroking fragile souls,
Driving them to chase hollow goals.

With head held high, oblivious and blind,
Proud hearts crave attention, endlessly pined.
They crave recognition, a pedestal to claim,
Yet fail to see the damage left in their aim.

Like a towering mountain, they stand so tall,
But on shaky grounds, they eventually fall.
For pride, oh, how it deceives and betrays,
Leading astray on treacherous, prideful ways.

Presumption and arrogance, pride's companions,
Deafening humility's gentle companions.
They lord over others with haughty disdain,
Basking in false glory, causing others pain.

Ah, pride, the deadliest sin of them all,
With its allure, it beckons, its victims enthralled.
It blinds the wise and rots the noble heart,
Tearing apart friendships, ripping souls apart.

A humble heart, free from pride's wicked chains,
Finds joy in modesty, where true honour reigns.
Let us learn from the errors of those who've lost,
For in genuine humility, lies wisdom's utmost.

So, let us tread carefully, with hearts sincere,
Avoiding pride's snare, with its path unclear.
For in its grasp, we risk losing what is pure,
And find solace in virtues that endure.

The 7 Deadly Sins- Sloth

In the realm of vices, where shadows lurk,
Resides a sin, a lethargic quirk.
Sloth, slow and seductive, a tempting vice,
An indulgence that offers no heed or advice.

Oh, Sloth, you ensnare with your tranquil embrace,
Lulling souls into a slovenly haze.
In idleness, time lazily unwinds,
As ambition and purpose remain far behind.

The sluggard, confined to a static dwell,
Where laziness thrives and motivation quells.
Tasks undone, dreams deferred, cast aside,
As Sloth's grip tightens, companionship denied.

With heavy eyelids and a torpid heart,
Sloth whispers sweet seduction, tearing souls apart.
Days blend into nights in a drowsy embrace,
Lost in the haze of exhaustion and .

But beware, dear souls if Sloth's chains you embrace,
For stagnation and regret shall take their place.
Ambition will wither, dreams left unfulfilled,
As Sloth consumes, leaving hearts empty and stilled.

Oh, Sloth, you temptress of languid stead,
Eating away at the core of our thread,
For in your grip, life slowly decays,
Leaving naught but regret and wasted days.

So rise from this slumber, break free from your ties,
Shake off the shackles with passionate cries.
Embrace the vigour that pulses within,
For life's wonders await those who dare to begin.

Break free from Sloth's clasp, let ambition ignite,
Spark a fire within, let it burn, shining bright.
For in the pursuit of purpose and zest,
We find the true meaning, the path that is best.

The 7 Deadly Sins- Wrath

In every soul, a darkness dwells,
A rage that burns, like fiery hells.
It twists and turns, unleashing wrath,
A tempest storm, on freedom's path.

Beware the wrath, with its eyes ablaze,
Its fury deep, in fiery rays.
It seeks revenge, with vengeful might,
A thirst for power, to ignite.

The sin of wrath, a deadly vice,
It consumes all, like rolling dice.
It tears apart, both young and old,
Unleashing chaos, unrestrained and bold.

With clenched fists and tightened jaw,
Wrath escalates, breaking the law.
Destroying friendships, tearing hearts,
Leaving behind shattered, broken parts.

In moments of anger, reason lost,
Impulsive acts, at any cost.
The fires of wrath, they burn and sear,
Leaving behind regret and fear.

THE SEVEN HEAVENLY VIRTUES

The 7 Heavenly Virtues- Charity

In realms above, where angels soar,
A virtue pure, forever more,
Charity, a light divine,
A beacon in this world's design.

With open heart and arms outstretched,
To those in need, a friend, a fetch.
She gives with love, with boundless grace,
And helps the lost find their true place.

With bounteous care, she tends to pain,
A soothing touch, a gentle rain.
She heals the wounds, both seen and hidden,
Her words a solace, sorrow ridden.

In times of strife, of deep despair,
She offers hope, beyond compare.
With selfless acts and silent grace,
She paints a brighter, fairer space.

She sees the world through tender eyes,
Discovers joy in others' sighs.
The simplest act, a heartfelt gift,
Her presence, makes the spirits always lift.

From humble acts to grand displays,
Charity fills our darkest days.
In giving love, we find our worth,
Our souls redeemed upon this earth.

The 7 Heavenly Virtues- Chastity

In realms divine where virtues shine,
One stands out with a grace sublime.
Chastity, a virtue pure and bright,
Guiding souls through day and night.

Within thy heart, a sacred flame,
Preserving virtue, full of aim.
Thy noble spirit, untamed desire,
Bathing in purity, rising higher.

In duty bound, you hold the key,
To keep thy passions in unity.
Avoiding temptations of the worldly pleasures,
Chastity guards thy hidden treasures.

Oh, let this virtue be your shield,
As battles fierce, it shall reveal
The strength to resist, the power to choose,
Chastity, in you, forever infused.

In love's embrace, let chastity guide,
A tender bond that will not subside.
With reverence and patience, it will survive,
A love that blossoms, pure and alive.

Cherish the body, a temple divine,
In modesty, may your spirit align.
For in chastity's embrace, you'll find,
A peace of mind, serene and kind.

Oh Chastity, an eternal flame,
With pure intentions and no shame.
In thy grace, we find liberation,
A virtue revered, without hesitation.

The 7 Heavenly Virtues- Diligence

In the realm of virtues, one soars supreme,
A quality of character, strong and gleam.
Diligence, relentless pursuit of striving,
A beacon of focus, always thriving.

With unwavering effort, it takes its stand,
A mighty force that guides, like a steady hand.
In every endeavour, it goes beyond measure,
A virtue so grand, a precious treasure.

Diligence sings a song of consistent endeavour,
Embracing challenges, it will never sever.
A tireless worker, never one to rest,
It rises above obstacles, passes every test.

Like a bee gathering nectar, diligent it appears,
Building its dreams, conquering all fears.
In tedious tasks, it finds purpose and meaning,
With grit and perseverance, the goal intervening.

In classrooms and workshops, where knowledge blooms,
Diligence shines brightly, breaking through gloom.
The student thrives, fuelled by passion's fire,
Seeking growth, climbing higher and higher.

In business and labour, where success is sought,
Diligence graces those who work and have fought.
The entrepreneur, courageous in their venture,
Faces setbacks and risks, but never will censure.

In relationships blooming, with love and care,
Diligence nurtures, a commitment rare.
Through ups and downs, it holds steadfast,
Building foundations that will forever last.

In service and kindness, diligence serves,
A hand that reaches out, compassion observes.
The world is enriched by its selfless giving,
A virtue so pure, a way of truly living.

In moral decisions, where right and wrong reside,
Diligence aligns with truth, its moral compass tied.
It walks a path of honour, never straying,
Upholding integrity, its belief never swaying.

The 7 Heavenly Virtues- Gratitude

In a world of moments, big and small,
Where blessings bloom and hearts enthral,
There shines a virtue, pure and bright,
Gratitude, an inner guiding light.

With humble heart and open soul,
Gratitude, its spirit whole,
It whispers thanks for every day,
For fortunes, blessings that come our way.

When the sun rises with golden gleam,
Gratitude cherishes its vibrant beam,
For every dawn and nature's grace,
For miracles woven in time and space.

In bounteous harvest, fields of green,
Gratitude dances in the serene,
For food that nourishes body and mind,
For abundance, our spirits entwined.

In laughter shared amid close friends,
Gratitude smiles and joyously sends,
For fellowship and love sincere,
For kindred spirits always near.

In cherished family bonds so tight,
Gratitude glows, a warming light,
For love unending, through thick and thin,
For the ties that bind from deep within.

In sorrow's shadow, in life's despair,
Gratitude whispers, a solace rare,
For lessons learned from trials endured,
For strength rebuilt, and spirits reassured.

In random acts of kindness shown,
Gratitude blossoms, its seeds sown,
For hearts that give without asking why,
For compassion's touch, a love so high.

Gratitude, a virtue to be embraced,
In every moment, each breath embraced,
For life's symphony, a melody in tune,
Gratitude's chorus, a celestial boon.

The 7 Heavenly Virtues- Humility

In towering realms where virtues reside,
A noble virtue, humility, abides.
A gentle whisper amid life's stride,
A cherished trait, where hearts confide.

Humility, a humble sword it does wield,
In gracious ways, its strength revealed.
Not seeking praise or power's yield,
But serving others with love unsealed.

Like a river, flowing with serene grace,
Humility shines in every embrace.
It nurtures hearts, leaving no trace,
Of arrogance or pride to deface.

In the face of success, it remains steadfast,
Not swayed by glory or momentary blast.
A beacon of humbleness, it will always last,
A virtue that's timeless, from the past.

It cherishes wisdom, in truth it thrives,
In quiet actions, its essence survives.
With selfless acts, it constantly strives,
To lift others up, as it gently arrives.

Where egos shrink, humility grows,
An inner strength that eternally flows.
It humbles the mighty, it enlightens the chose,
A virtue that blossoms wherever it shows

The 7 Heavenly Virtues- Patience

In a world so fast-paced, where haste takes control,
There lies a virtue, serene and whole.
Patience, dear patience, a guiding light,
Leading souls to peace, through the darkest night.

Like a calm river, flowing gently and slow,
Patience teaches hearts, how to let go.
In the face of adversity, it stands tall,
A mighty fortress, unyielding to the fall.

With every tick of time, it whispers to the soul,
To breathe and to wait, for the perfect whole.
For patience is a gift, a tranquil embrace,
A virtue that elevates, with exquisite grace.

In the trials of life, when storms may arise,
Patience is the anchor, that keeps us wise.
It soothes our restless hearts, like a healing balm,
Guiding us through chaos, with a soothing calm.

When dreams are distant, and goals seem far away,
Patience stirs hope, and nurtures our way.
For in the waiting, new chapters unfold,
And miracles blossom, tales yet untold.

Patience, a teacher with endless insight,
Teaching us acceptance, through its gentle might.
For it understands, the beauty of delay,
And the wisdom that comes, with every passing day.

The 7 Heavenly Virtues- Temperance

In a realm where virtues reside,
Temperance, pure and dignified,
A beacon of serene control,
An emblem of a balanced soul.

Tempering the flames of desire,
With restraint, it does inspire,
To rein in every wayward whim,
Embrace harmony, on a whim.

In our lives, a guiding light,
Through turbulent storms, dark as night,
Temperance fosters inner peace,
And helps all our struggles to cease.

In the realm of excess and greed,
Temperance calls, with gentle plead,
To banish gluttony's embrace,
And find contentment in each space.

With moderation at its core,
Temperance opens wisdom's door,
Bridging the gap between extremes,
Guiding us to fulfil our dreams.

In moments of anger, it whispers calm,
Leads us away from needless harm,
Imparting patience, like a balm,
With Temperance, we stay strong and warm.

Temperance knows when to retreat,
To navigate life's winding fleet,
Amidst indulgence or despair,
It teaches us how to repair.

For in its virtue, we shall find,
A strength of spirit, unconfined,
To face the chaos that may arise,
With temperate grace, it harmonizes.

A Letter To My Future Self
Never Give Up Because Great Things Take Time

Dear Future Me, In A Distant Time,
In struggles hard, in uphill climb,
Remember this, do not forget,
Great things take time, don't you fret.

When shadows loom and doubts arise,
Look to the skies, where hope lies.
Your dreams are valid, bright and true,
Each step you take, you will renew.

Though storms may rage and winds may howl,
Hold fast, stay true, wear the courage's cowl.
For in the depths of the darkest night,
Lies strength within, a shining light.

Embrace each challenge, face each fear,
For growth comes near when victory's near.
Your path is long, your journey grand,
So never give up, you'll understand.

So write these words upon your heart,
Let them guide you, never apart.
For greatness waits, it's yours to claim,
Stay resilient, ignite your flame.

With patience as your steadfast guide,
Unfurl your wings, let doubts subside.
And in the end, you will find,
The treasures of a patient mind.

So hold on tight, dear future self,
Embrace the journey, embrace yourself.
For great things come to those who wait,
Your time will come, it's not too late.

A Soul Unseen

I hope that someday when I am gone,
Someone, somewhere, picks my soul up,
Off these pages, where my words live on,
And in their heart, they feel the love's gallop.

For I have poured my essence, deep and true,
In each line, every verse I have penned,
A tapestry of emotions, woven askew,
Hoping my words touch hearts till the end.

In the vast expanse of literary grace,
I yearn for my spirit to be embraced,
By a gentle reader, with eyes of solace.

To know that my words have kindled a flame,
Within a soul unknown, yet forever claimed,
I pray, "I would've loved her," they exclaim.

So let my soul be lifted from these pages,
And let it soar on the wings of time,
May its essence transcend the passing ages,
A testament to love's infinite prime.

For in the realm of words, forever free,
A connection formed, beyond what we see,
I hope someday, my soul finds empathy.

May it evoke emotions, both soft and fierce,
Stirring hearts to ponder, reflect, and muse,
And in that moment, my spirit will pierce,

The boundaries of life, where love ensues.
For in the echoes of my written art,
I long to touch a soul, light up a heart,
And leave a legacy that won't depart.

Be Loud About The Things That Are Important To You

In a world where silence reigns,
Speak up, let your voice unchain.
Be loud about what stirs your soul,
Let your passions take control.

Raise your voice against injustice,
Let it echo, let it thrust.
For the causes that truly matter,
Be the voice that makes them scatter.

Don't cower in the shadows deep,
Let your convictions rise and leap.
Shout out for the ones in need,
Your words, a powerful seed.

Be the thunder in the quiet night,
Illuminate the darkness with all your might.
For the things that make you whole,
Be loud, be bold, speak from your soul.

Beauty Is Dangerous, But Intelligence Is Lethal

In a world where beauty dances with grace,
Beware, for it can be a deceiving embrace.
For like a rose with its thorns so keen,
Gorgeous exteriors may conceal something unseen.

But it is intelligence that strikes with might,
A force, a power, that shines through the night.
For in the realm where knowledge takes flight,
It can illuminate paths once hidden from sight.

Oh, the danger of beauty can often mesmerize,
But it is intelligence that truly paralyze.
For words wielded with intellect and precision,
Can bring down even the mightiest of visions.

A pretty face may captivate a crowd,
But an intelligent mind can silence them loud.
With logic, reason, and a thirst for more,
It's intelligence that opens wisdom's door.

So let us not be swayed by beauty's ruse,
Nor underestimate what intelligence can choose.
For beauty may entrance, but intelligence is lethal,
With its capacity to shape the world in a single sequel.

Being A Hero Doesn't Mean You're Invincible. It Just Means That You're Brave Enough To Stand Up And Do What's Needed

~Heroes of Olympus: Mark of Athena
In fields of battle, where the bravest dare not tread
There stands a hero, with a heart full of dread
For though they may be strong, their fears they do not hide
But face them head on, with courage by their side

With every step they take, they risk their own life
Yet still they press on, for justice and what is right
They know not victory, but only strife
Yet still they fight, with all their might

For being a hero doesn't mean you're invincible
It just means that you're brave enough to stand tall
To face the challenges that others cannot bear
And rise above the trials that come your way

They face the unknown with steady nerve,
And never falter, no matter the curve,
For they know that every challenge can be met,
If they stand strong and never retreat.

Books

"Why do you read books?" they inquire,
Asking me why I desire
To stray from the world's harsh decree,
From life's cruel, bitter reality.

I reply with a steady voice and air,
As I speak, trying to make them aware,
For within those pages, a refuge I find,
A solace, a haven, a peace of mind.

In the grip of words, I can wander free,
Exploring vast worlds, as far as I see.
Through thrilling tales, I can soar and fly,
Unburdened by sorrow, no need to cry.

Books embrace me, warming my heart,
Transporting my soul, setting me apart.
In their gentle embrace, I find solace and peace,
A respite from life's struggles and ceaseless grease.

When darkness surrounds, when life seems unclear,
Books light the path, erasing all fear.
Characters become friends, their stories my own,
Their trials and triumphs, forever known.

Books possess the magic to ease all my strife,
To unveil new perspectives, to broaden my life.
They teach me compassion, courage, and grace,
To embrace diversity, the world's vibrant face.

So, when they ask me, "Why do you read?"
I say, with gratitude, without any need,
"Books are my sanctuary, my saving grace,
My escape from reality's desolate space."

With hearts now enlightened, they start to see,
The power and beauty of books, just like me.
For in those precious pages, we can all find,
An escape, a refuge, for hearts intertwined.

Childhood

In childhood's realm of endless dreams,
Where teddy bears held all their schemes,
We danced through fields with joy untamed,
A world of wonder where we aimed.

The sun-lit days, so full of glee,
Imagination ran wild and free,
Climbing trees with nimble grace,
Lost in games of hide and chase.

We laughed and cried, both loud and clear,
With friends so close, forever near,
Building sandcastles by the shore,
With dreams of adventures to explore.

In childhood's realm of make-believe,
We sailed the seas, on make-shift seas,
With pirate hats upon our heads,
We charted paths where treasure spreads.

The stars above, like sparkling charms,
Guided us through night's loving arms,
Dreams took flight as we closed our eyes,
Eager for morning's sweet surprise.

Oh, childhood days so pure and bright,
Filled with innocence and sheer delight,
Oh, how we yearn to go back again,
To feel that joy, that freedom reign.

But though we grow and time goes by,
That precious child still dwells inside,
And through life's windings, we shall see,
The child within will always be.

Confusion

My confusion, a maze of the mind
A labyrinth of thoughts, so hard to find
The path unclear, the way obscure
A haze of doubts, a mist of pure

In this tangled web of uncertainty
I search for answers, but they flee
Like shadows in the night, they escape
Leaving me lost, in a daze

My heart races, my soul astray
As I try to find my way
Through the thick fog of disarray
Where truth and lies, they slay

The questions mount, the answers few
My mind awhirl, in a spin
I seek the light, the truth to view
But it eludes me, like a mirage in the dew

In this state of confusion, I stand
A stranger in a foreign land
With no map, no compass, no guide
Just the echoes of my own cries

Do You Ever Miss The Old You?

Do you ever miss the old you,
The one with dreams so fresh and true?
When life was simple, skies were blue,
Before the world changed its hue.

Those days of innocence and grace,
Before time sped up its pace,
When laughter filled each empty space,
And worries had no trace.

Do you ever long to find
The peace left in your mind,
When life was gentle, sweet, and kind,
And joys were easy to unwind?

Don't Adapt The Energy In The Room.
Influence The Energy In The Room.

In the dance of life, in a subtle sway,
Don't blend in shadows, but find your own way.
Amidst the thrum of whispered gloom,
Stand tall, ignite, and brightly bloom.

Don't adapt to currents, meek and tame,
Be the spark that lights the flame.
Influence the energy, bold and true,
Let your spirit shine on through.

With words that echo, hearts entwine,
Craft a melody, make it divine.
Paint the air with hues that gleam,
Inspire, create, fulfil the dream.

So as you journey through each day,
Remember, dear one, in every way—
Don't adapt the energy in the room,
Be the force that breaks the gloom.

Don't Fashion Me Into A Maiden That Needs Saving From A Dragon For I Am The Dragon.

In fiery depths where shadows dance,
I rise, a dragon in a daring stance.
Don't weave me into tales forlorn,
Where maidens weep from dusk 'til morn.

Strength courses through my beating heart,
Flames fierce, a symphony, an art.
No saviour sought, no knight in gleam,
For I am both reality and dream.

Do not mold me in fragile guise,
To fit the world's restrictive ties.
Embrace my scales, my fierce pride,
In shadows deep, where truths abide.

I breathe my fire, unbridled and free,
A force of nature, wild as the sea.
So don't fashion me in roles untrue,
For I am the dragon—I am you.

Don't Worry Mother, Your Daughter Is A Soldier

Don't worry, mother, I've grown bolder,
In the storms of life, I am a soldier.
Through battles fought, my spirit's ignited,
With iron will, I won't be slighted.

In this world, where chaos may smother,
I stand tall, armed with strength like no other.
Unyielding, I face each challenge anew,
With every step, I prove my love is true.

Through darkest nights and shadows unknown,
I'll never falter, I'll never be alone.
My heart beats strong, a warrior's cadence,
With every breath, I embrace my essence.

Through raging fires and mountains impassable,
I conquer fears, forever unassailable.
No enemy can dent my soul's armour,
For I'm your daughter, a determined charmer.

Though storms may rage and winds may howl,
Within my core, an unbreakable scowl.
I march forth, a valiant soldier unwavering,
For love and honour, I am unwavering.

So don't worry, mother, in my stride,
You'll find the strength I cannot hide.
With love as my shield, my sword held high,
Together, we'll conquer, beyond the sky.

Everyone Says Follow Your Heart But If My Heart Is In A Trillion Pieces
Which Piece Do I Follow?

In a world full of voices, each one a cacophony,
Everyone says follow your heart, but what if it's broken?
If my heart is in a trillion pieces, which one do I choose?
Do I follow the pieces that whisper sweet nothings, or the ones that sting like a bruise?

Maybe I should follow the piece that beats for love,
The one that yearns for adventure, for something new.
But what if that piece is shattered, lost in the fray?
Then what do I do, when my heart is gone astray?

Perhaps I should heed the piece that whispers calm,
The one that urges patience, and a gentle balm.
But what if that piece is drowned out by the noise?
Then how can I find my way, through the chaotic noise?

Forever Writing A Story In My Head

Forever writing, in my mind's vast expanse,
A story unfolds, in an endless dance.
Characters crafted with intricate grace,
Each step they take, a new path they trace.

Words like brushstrokes on a canvas unseen,
A world of my making, where I am queen.
Plot twists and turns, like a winding stream,
In the landscape of dreams, reality may seem.

Pages unfurl with passing thought,
In the tapestry of tales, my essence is caught.
Emotions laid bare, in black ink and white,
A symphony of words, dancing in the light.

Forever writing, my story goes on,
In the chambers of my mind, till the break of dawn.
A never-ending saga, a creative spree,
This story I write, will forever be me.

Global Warming

Global Warming, a burning concern,
Do we heed the lessons we should learn?
Ice caps melting, oceans rise,
Are we blind to the nature's cries?

Forests vanishing, creatures fade,
Do we see the price we've paid?
Heatwaves scorching lands once green,
Have we lost what could have been?

Hurricanes rage with greater might,
Do we ignore our planet's plight?
Species lost at rapid pace,
Can we afford this reckless race?

Carbon clouds dim skies above,
Is this the legacy of our love?
Future generations left to bear,
Will they forgive the scars we share?

Questions linger, answers sought,
Must we act as time grows short?
Global warming's urgent call,
Shall we rise or watch it fall?

Go On With What Your Heart Tells You, Or You Will Lose All.

~Percy Jackson: The Lightening Thief

In life's grand tapestry of time and fate,
We each must choose our own unique path,
For those who heed their hearts, fortune waits,
But those who hesitate may forever lack.

The whispers of our souls guide us along,
To seek our dreams and sing our songs,
For in our passions lie our strength,
And in our fears, our greatest length.

So let not doubts and doubters hold you back,
Nor let the voices of others make you crack,
For it is only when we dare to try,
That we can truly reach for the sky.

When love and joy ignite our way,
We find the courage to pursue the day,
For though the road ahead may seem unclear,
Our hearts know where we need to steer.

So go on with what your heart tells you,
And never let your spirit falter too,
For if you follow your inner light,
Your journey will be bright and just right.

Good Friends Don't Let You Do Stupid Things Alone

In life's grand journey, through highs and lows,
There's a guiding light, a love that truly shows,
For good friends, like beacons, they always share,
They won't let you stumble; they'll always be there.

When temptation whispers its enticing song,
And foolishness seeks to steer you wrong,
A true companion, with wisdom pure,
Will lend a hand, and make you endure.

With heartfelt laughter, they keep you sane,
In moments of madness, they ease the strain,
They join in the madness, with glee and delight,
But also remind you, to do what's right.

They embrace your quirks, your flaws and all,
And to your dreams, they devoutly call,
Through thick and thin, their loyalty's true,
Good friends guard you, like a shield that grew.

For in unity, strength and courage reside,
They chase away shadows, eliminate pride,
They stand by your side, no matter the test,
And never let you face stupidness alone, at best.

Through wild adventures, they're your willing guide,
In mischievous endeavours, they'll never hide,
They take your hand, and dance by the fire,
Together conquering life, they'll never tire.

For good friends, in their bond, find delight,
Protecting you like warriors, day, and night,
They hold your hand, when the path is unclear,
Guiding you forward, calming your fear.

So cherish those friends, who illuminate your way,
With their presence, making brighter each day,
For in this world, where moments are rare,
Good friends ensure you never stumble, never scare.

Her Life Changed When She Learned The Monsters Were Protecting Her

In shadows deep where fears reside,
She found a truth, no longer to hide.
Monsters lurking, misunderstood,
Guardians in the dark, where they stood.

Her life transformed with newfound sight,
Monsters' presence now shining bright.
Their claws and fangs, not meant to harm,
But shields against a world's alarm.

Whispers of solace, unseen embrace,
Monsters shielding, in every space.
Guiding her through daunting nights,
Embracing darkness, revealing lights.

No longer alone in the endless night,
Monsters by her side, shining so bright.
Protectors, defenders, in disguise,
Her heart now sings, reaching the skies.

Hope

Every night we close our eyes,
With no guarantee of sunrise,
Yet hope resides within our hearts,
As we prepare for morning's start.

A slumber deep, where dreams may bring,
A glimpse of what tomorrow brings,
But with uncertainty we rest,
And trust that fate will know what's best.

We set our alarms, loud and clear,
To awaken us, without a fear,
For in our sleep, we place our trust,
That hope will guide us, it is a must.

For life's a gamble, every day,
Yet still we rise, come what may,
We face the world with open eyes,
Embracing hope, the sun will rise.

In darkness, hope is our beacon bright,
Guiding us through the deepest night,
For in that simple alarm's sound,
We sense the promise, hope is found.

Though life is fragile, and unknown,
Hope keeps our spirits brightly sown,
It lends us strength to face each morn,
With faith that new opportunities are born.

So every night, as we lie in bed,
Hope whispers softly in our head,
Promising a chance to strive,
To keep on dreaming, being alive.

And as we wake to a brand-new day,
Hope blooms within, showing the way,
For though uncertainty may remain,
Hope assures us life is worth the pain.

How Does It Feel Like? To Be A Man?

In a world where faith abounds,
Where beliefs in me resound,
As a girl, I yearn to be seen,
To break the chains, to intervene.

Running fast with every stride,
Seeking acceptance far and wide,
Would my journey meet no strife,
If I were but a man in life?

Oh, the weight upon my chest,
The doubts that never rest,
Sick of proving worth and skill,
Yearning for equality's thrill.

When everyone believes ya,
Without judgment, without a plea,
To stand tall, unburdened, free,
What's that like? Pray, tell me.

But I'll endure, I'll keep the pace,
For change must come at any case,
With strength and courage, I will strive,
To break the barriers, to truly thrive.

For all the girls who dream aloud,
A future bright, where they're endowed,
We'll rewrite the tale, shift the plan,
Embrace unity, woman, and man.

I Am Not Afraid Of Storms,
For I Am Learning How To Sail My Ship

~Lousia May Alcott

Oh, the wind it howls and the waves they crash,
As the tempest rages on in its wrath.
But fear not, dear heart, for I have found
A secret to tame the wild blue sea profound.

I've learned to harness the gale's great might,
To ride the swells and dance with delight.
My vessel, strong and sturdy as steel,
Cuts through the foam, unyielding and real.

With every wave that crashes high,
I feel alive, my spirit soaring sky-high.
For though the storm may rage and roar,
I know that I can conquer more.

So let the winds blow fierce and strong,
And let the lightning flash all night long.
For in the eye of every storm,
Lies peace, wisdom, and a wondrous form.

In these turbulent waters, I find grace,
And learn to navigate by faith.
For when the tempest rages most,
It teaches me to trust, to stand tall and boast.

So bring on the gales, the thunder and rain,
For in each storm, I find a friend again.
I am not afraid, no, not at all,
For I am learning how to sail my ship, standing tall.

I Feel Small, But So Are Stars From A Distance

In the vast expanse where dreams take flight,
I feel small beneath the cloak of night.
Yet stars above, in their cosmic dance,
Twinkle softly, beckoning a glance.

From afar, they seem but specks of light,
Glimmering jewels in the velvet night.
Their distant glow, a timeless trance,
A reminder of life's grand expanse.

Though I am tiny, a mere mote of dust,
In the universe's symphony, I trust.
For just like stars in their brilliance,
I too hold a spark of resilience.

So as I gaze at the skies above,
I find solace in this truth, this love:
Though small I may be in this vast expanse,
My light shines bright, in cosmic dance.

I Know I'm Young But My Mind Is Well Beyond My Years

I know I'm young but my mind is well beyond
My years, a vessel of wisdom untamed,
A soul unburdened by life's heavy bond,
In realms of thought, my spirit unconstrained.

Though youth's embrace may cloak my tender frame,
Within, a universe of knowledge blooms,
The boundless depths of understanding tame,
As wisdom's light within my heart consumes.

No chains of time can hold my dreams at bay,
For in my mind, the ages intertwine,
I dance with sages of a bygone day,
And seek profound truths that mortals may find.

So let me wander in these realms unseen,
For though I'm young, my mind is ever keen.

I Still Repeat The Things You Said To Me In My Head

In echoes of memory, your words resound,
Whispers cling to me, a haunting sound.
Each phrase, the melody, lingers in my mind,
Captured moments of a kinder time.

I still repeat the things you said to me,
A bittersweet chorus, a melancholic decree.
Like fragile petals caught in the wind's embrace,
Your words drift, leaving a wistful trace.

Promises made in whispers soft and true,
Now fragments of a past I once knew.
They dance and linger, refusing to depart,
Etched in the chambers of my tender heart.

Amidst the silence, your voice softly rings,
A symphony of echoes, where longing sings.
I hold onto each word, a cherished token,
In the quiet hours, they remain unbroken.

Though time may pass and memories fade,
Your words endure, in shadows unswayed.
I still repeat the things you said to me,
An eternal echo of what used to be.

I Was Born To Tell Stories

I was born to tell stories, weave tales untold,
In whispers of wonder, in words that unfold.
From the depths of my soul, I paint with my pen,
Crafting worlds unseen, where dreams find their den.

Each character breathes, each plot takes its flight,
Through valleys of sorrow, and peaks of delight.
My heart spills its ink on the canvas of time,
In rhythms and rhymes, a lyrical chime.

In ancient traditions, my purpose defined,
To capture the essence of humankind's mind.
Through laughter and tears, through struggles and glories,
I dance with the muses, revealing life's stories.

I Write Because I Don't Know What I Think Until I Read What I Say.

In words I find my wandering mind's true way,
I write to trace the thoughts that in me lay.
For in the lines, my tangled musings play,
Revealing truths I didn't know today.

A dance of letters on the blank expanse,
Each phrase a mirror of my inner glance.
Through ink and paper, thoughts begin to dance,
Revealing depths of thought in their advance.

I write to peel the layers of my soul,
To find the parts that make my being whole.
In scribbled words, my essence finds its role,
Unveiling mysteries, making me feel whole.

So pen in hand, I let my feelings flow,
Discovering the things I didn't know.
In writing's embrace, my mind can grow,
"I write," I say, "to truly let me know."

I Wrote A Poem About It, And Then Threw It Away

In solitude, I penned a verse so true,
Expressing depths of feelings, old and new.
Yet in a moment's doubt, it met its fate—
Torn asunder, cast off to abate.

For what use are words in a one-sided plea?
To hearts unmoved, they offer no decree.
No solace found in lines that go astray,
Unseen by eyes that glance the other way.

Why dedicate to those who never see,
Or echo back with reciprocity?
Silent souls hold secrets close, untold,
Leaving poets' hearts in heavy cold.

Thus, I dispose of my unwritten plea,
Releasing ties that bind and set me free.
No more shall ink spill for the deafened ear,
A silent vow to self, crystal clear.

If I Disappear... Will You Look For Me?

If I disappear on a mist-laden night,
Will you search for my whispers in the pale moonlight?
Through the echoes of time, in shadows so deep,
Will you follow the traces of promises to keep?

In the stillness of moments, lost and unseen,
Will you seek out the remnants of where I have been?
Amongst fading footprints on shores of the sea,
Will you find me in memories, wild and free?

When the winds carry secrets of dreams untold,
Will you listen for echoes that never grow old?
In the heart's silent chambers, a soft melody,
Will you remember the essence of you and me?

If I disappear into the vast unknown,
Will you hold onto fragments of love we've sown?
In the tapestry woven with threads of our fate,
Will you wait by the doorway, before it's too late?

If You Could Read My Mind, You'd Know How Hard I Tried

If you could read my mind, dear friend,
You'd know how hard I tried to mend,
The broken pieces of my soul,
The battles fought, the stories untold.

In quiet nights with tears unspoken,
I forged ahead, my spirit unbroken,
Through trials fierce and burdens carried,
A warrior's heart, yet often weary.

If you could see the scars I conceal,
Etched deep within, wounds that won't heal,
You'd witness strength in every stride,
That keeps me going, side by side.

With every stumble, I rise again,
Determined to conquer, to transcend,
For within this heart there lies a fire,
Defying limits, reaching higher.

In dreams pursued and hopes embraced,
A testament to the challenges faced,
Each failure a lesson deeply learned,
Fuel for the fire that ever burns.

If you could read my mind, you'd find,
Resilience born from a restless mind,
A relentless pursuit to touch the sky,
To soar on wings, unhindered, high.

So judge me not by what you see,
But by the battles fought silently,
For if you could read my mind and soul,
You'd know the strength that makes me whole.

I'm Gonna Say "I Got This,"
Even With Tears In My Eyes

In times of trial and heartache, I'll stand tall and proud,
Though tears may fall like rain, I'll never let my spirit bow.
I'll grit my teeth and bear the pain, and through it all, I'll say,
"I got this," with a fierce determination, day by day.

My eyes may well up with tears, but I'll wipe them away,
For I know that strength lies not in never falling, but in getting up again.
I'll draw on every ounce of courage I possess, and rise above the fray,
And with a defiant cry of "I got this," I'll face each new day.

So let the world around me tremble and quake,
For I am a warrior, with a heart that refuses to shake.
I'll stand tall and proud, no matter what life brings,
And with every tear I cry, I'll shout out "I got this" with wings.

I'm Not In This World To Live Up To Your Expectations And You're Not In This World To Live Up To Mine

In a world where expectations reign,
I am not here to meet your gain.
Defined not by what you seek,
My path is mine, unique and sleek.

Your standards, they do not bind,
For your journey is not intertwined with mine.
We walk our paths, distinct and free,
No need to conform, no need to agree.

Let judgments fade, let pressures go,
In this vast world, we ebb and flow.
A reminder clear, for you and me,
We're not here to live up to each other's decree.

Embrace the differences, let them shine,
For in diversity, beauty we find.
In this vast tapestry, colours entwine,
I'll be true to me, and you to thine.

Imagination

In a land where dreams do flow,
Imagination starts to show,
A world of wonder, vast and free,
Where anything can come to be.

Here the clouds are cotton candy,
And rivers flow with honeyed glee,
Mountains soar and touch the sky,
While colours twinkle in the eye.

Creatures dance in graceful flight,
With wings as shimmering as moonlight,
Faeries whisper secrets in the breeze,
While unicorns graze among the trees.

Imagination paints the perfect scene,
Of meadows green and skies serene,
Where fireflies light the velvety night,
And stars create a symphony of light.

Through the realms of make-believe we explore,
Casting aside what we think we know,
Imagination, an endless portal unfurled,
To transport us to another world.

With boundless magic and endless delight,
In this dimension, where dreams take flight,
Imagination sets our spirit free,
To wander in lands of possibility.

So close your eyes and let your mind soar,
To realms where wonders galore,
With imagination as our guide and charioteer,
Another world is yours, my dear.

In The End, We Will Remember Not The Words Of Our Enemies, But The Silence Of Our Friends

In echoes of time, memories descend,
We recall not the foes' piercing words they send.
Rather, it's the hush of friends, so serene,
Their silence profound, in moments unseen.

When shadows lengthen and troubles amass,
It's not the harsh jibes that linger, alas.
But the quiet support, steadfast and true,
A word left unspoken, yet deeply imbued.

In the tapestry of life, woven threads of care,
The absence of sound, a bond we share.
For when words fail and actions transcend,
In silence, our friends, their love they extend.

So in the end, when recollections blend,
Not the enemies' clamour, but friendships defend.
The silence speaks volumes, a tale to transcend,
In hearts and in minds, forever to mend.

In The End... We'll All Become Memories

In the end, when shadows grow long and deep,
We all become tales that memories keep.
Whispers of laughter, tears shed in the night,
Echo through time, like stars shining bright.

Each life a chapter, a page in the book,
Filled with adventures wherever we look.
Stories of triumph, of loss and of love,
Written in stars by the heavens above.

Our journeys entwined, like rivers that flow,
Through valleys of joy, through mountains of woe.
In the end, we're but words on the page,
Bound by the past, yet free as a sage.

So live your story with passion and grace,
Embrace every moment, in every place.
For in the end, when all is said and done,
We'll be remembered for how we have spun

The threads of our lives into tales so grand,
Woven with care by each heart and hand.
And though we may part from this earthly domain,
Our stories will linger, forever to remain

Is It My Fault Though?

In shadows deep, where doubts do grow,
I ponder in the night's soft glow,
Whispers haunting like a woe—
Is it my fault, this ebb and flow?

Through trials fierce, my spirit soars,
Yet burdened by unseen wars,
Blaming self on distant shores—
Is it my fault, these unseen scars?

The mirror reflects a troubled gaze,
Lost in a labyrinthine maze,
Seeking solace in life's haze—
Is it my fault, these endless days?

Oh, tangled web of doubt and fear,
In heart's recess, you linger near,
Questioning all that I hold dear—
Is it my fault, this silent tear?

But hush now, inner voice unkind,
Within me, strength and light I find,
No burden is solely mine to bind—
Not my fault, but life entwined.

It's Not How Long You Live That Matters. It's What You Live For.

~Trials of Apollo: The Dark Prophecy
In life's fleeting hours, don't count the days,
For time is but a stream that flows away.
It's not the length of years that makes us stay,
But what we do with each moment we play.

A single breath can hold a lifetime's worth,
If filled with love, laughter, and dear earth.
So chase your dreams, let joy be your guide,
And make each day a masterpiece to reside.

Don't measure life by its final rest,
But by the memories that forever nest.
For it's the moments we cherish, the hearts we touch,
That give our lives their true meaning so much.

So live each day as if it were your last,
And fill your heart with beauty, grace, and passion at last.
For it's not how long you live that truly counts,
But what you live for that leaves a lasting stain on this world.

I've Lived A Thousand Lives And Loved A Thousand Loves. I've Walked On Distant Shores And Seen The End Of Time. Because I Read.

In realms of ink, I've danced the dance of fate,
A thousand lives embraced, a thousand loves elate.
Through pages turned, on shores both near and far,
I've glimpsed horizons grand, where endless stories s
par.

With each word consumed, time's veil unfurled,
To witness the end of days, yonder world unfurled.
For in the whispers of each written creed,
I found my solace true, my heart to heed.

In books, I voyaged far beyond the known,
Bridging realms of dreams, where truth is sown.
I've lived a thousand lives, loved a thousand more,
All because I dared to read—my spirit to explore.

Just Because I Don't Show It. Doesn't Mean I Don't Feel It.

In silence I bear a hidden weight,
Emotions deep, sealed by fate.
Just because I don't show it clear,
Doesn't mean there's no pain here.

Feelings dance in shadows cast,
A heart's whispers meant to last.
Though my mask may firmly seal,
Inside, raw emotions reel.

Quiet strength, a hidden art,
Concealing storms within my heart.
My soul, a canvas of unseen hues,
Painted with emotions I don't refuse.

Don't mistake my silence for lack,
Emotions simmer under guise, in fact.
Just because I don't let them spill,
Doesn't mean I can't feel, and always will.

Life Is Only Precious Because It Ends

~Heroes of Olympus: Son of Neptune
Life, oh life, a fleeting dream,
A fragile thing, a delicate scheme,
Precious moments, like grains of sand,
Slipping through our fingers, lost in demand.

We chase the hours, we race against time,
Our lives a canvas, ever-changing line,
Each day a stroke of brush, bold and free,
A masterpiece, waiting to be seen.

But life is precious, not just for its length,
Its value lies in its brevity and strength,
For in its end, we find our true worth,
And all that we hold dear on this earth.

So let us cherish each moment we share,
Let love and laughter fill the air,
For life may fade, but memories remain,
And the beauty of living will never wane.

Lillies

In gardens where the moonlight softly gleams,
Lilies dance in purity, fulfilling dreams.
Symbols of fertility, innocent and bright,
Their sweet beauty, a beacon of light.

Petals delicate, like whispers in the breeze,
Each bloom, a promise of life with ease.
Pure as dawn's first light, they stand tall,
Embodying nature's gentle call.

In their midst, rebirth quietly sings,
A sacred symbol of new beginnings.
Lilies grace the earth with their tender hue,
A testament to life's cycle, ever true.

May The Gods Have Mercy On My Enemies. Because I Won't.

May the gods have mercy on my foes, for I shall not show them any grace.

Their wicked deeds will bring their own doom, and they shall face my wrathful pace.

Their malice and deceit will turn upon themselves, like a sword in a circle of fire.

For I am one who will not be swayed by empty words or hollow desire.

My justice will prevail, and all who stand against me shall feel my ire.

So let the gods have mercy on my enemies, for I shall have none to spare.

Maybe... Maybe Forever Is A Word Meant For Memories, Not People...

Maybe forever is a distant land we seek,
Where memories reside, silent and meek.
In the tapestry of time, they gently sleep,
Whispering tales that make our hearts weep.

For people are fleeting, like shadows at dawn,
Transient souls in this world we spawn.
Yet memories linger, eternally bound,
In the fabric of existence, where echoes resound.

Maybe forever is a promise we make,
To cherish the moments that never forsake.
In the dance of life, where endings start,
Memories endure, etched in our heart.

So let us embrace what may not stay,
And hold onto memories, come what may.
For maybe forever is a word that we weave,
In the stories of our lives, where love will never leave.

My Thoughts Were Destroying Me.
I Tried Not To Think, But The Silence Was A Killer Too

My thoughts were destroying me, a maelstrom of despair,
A whirlwind of worry, a tempest of care.
I tried to repress them, to lock them away,
But the silence was a killer, a void to slay.

The quietude was a prison, a cell of my mind,
A place where my thoughts could not unwind.
The stillness was a torment, a never-ending plight,
A constant reminder of the darkness of night.

I yearned for the noise, the din of the day,
The hum of the city, the chatter of play.
For in the chaos, I found a strange peace,
A release from the prison of my own release.

But alas, the noise too was a foe,
A cacophony of sounds, a clamour to go.
It drowned out my thoughts, it stole my peace,
And left me with nothing but a sea of ceaseless ease.

Never Regret Anything That Made You Smile... Even If It's For A Short Period Of Time.

Don't fret the moments fleeting,
Smiles that make your heart start beating.
Embrace the joy, however brief,
Life's a mix of joy and grief.

A laugh, a grin, a moment shared,
In memories, these times are paired.
Cherish each smile, big or small,
They're the sweetest gifts of all.

Regrets fade when smiles endure,
Even if the moment's pure.
So let's savour each fleeting rhyme,
For those smiles make life sublime.

Nothing Is More Tragic Than Loving Someone To The Depths Of Your Soul Knowing They Cannot And Will Not Ever Love You Back.

~Trials of Apollo: The Hidden Oracle

In the darkest corners of my heart, I hide
A secret sorrow that cannot abide
For in my dreams, I see your face so bright
But know our love can never take flight

Your eyes, like stars, shine bright and true
But alas, their light cannot reach me too
For though my love for you may be pure and strong
It is not enough to last all life long

Oh, how I wish upon each passing day
That you could feel the same sweet way
But fate has other plans, it seems
And takes from me what it does not give

My love, a river wild and free
Cannot be tamed by destiny
Its currents crash against the shore
Leaving me lost forevermore

So here I stand, alone and apart
With a love that cannot find its heart
A tragic tale of unrequited desire
Forever etched within my mind's fire.

Poetry Doesn't Have To Rhyme, It Has To Touch Somewhere Your Hands Couldn't.

In the realm of words, a symphony unfolds,
Where lines unfurl and stories are told.
Poetry, not bound by rules or rhyme,
Weaves emotions in the fabric of time.

It reaches depths where the hands can't grasp,
Sculpting feelings that forever last.
Through verses whispered in silent plea,
It touches souls, sets imagination free.

Embracing shadows, painting light,
A canvas of thoughts taking flight.
In the heart of verse, where essence dwells,
Lies a magic that no tongue tells.

Push Yourself Because No One Else Is Going To Do It For You

In life's relentless stride, you'll find
No hand to hold, no easy ride.
Push yourself through doubt and fear,
Forge ahead, your purpose clear.

No one else can steer your way,
Through the trials of each new day.
Grit and strength must be your guide,
To conquer mountains, reach the sky wide.

Embrace the challenge, face the test,
In your heart, ignite the zest.
Push beyond what you once knew,
For greatness waits, it's up to you.

Rise above the noise and din,
Let determination be your kin.
Push yourself, with fire anew,
For the journey's end lies true.

Questions

In the realm of twilight's whisper,
Where shadows dance in the fading light,
Do dreams take flight on wings of wonder,
Or fade like stars in the morning's sight?

Does the river know its destined course,
As it winds through valleys deep and wide?
Do echoes carry tales untold,
Whispered secrets of the earth's long stride?

When the moon hangs low in the velvet sky,
Do the stars sing songs of ancient lore?
Is there a place where time stands still,
Where hearts find peace forevermore?

What lies beyond the edge of dawn,
Where the horizon meets the sky?
Are there answers to the questions asked,
Or do they float like clouds passing by?

In the tapestry of life's grand design,
Are we but players on a cosmic stage?
Do we hold the key to our own fate,
Or are we swept along by destiny's rage?

As we wander through this maze of existence,
Seeking truths that seem so far away,
Do we find solace in the unknown,
Or do the questions lead us astray?

Raise Your Words Not Your Voice

In a world of clamour and strife,
Where anger and fury run rife,
A gentle reminder, a guiding choice,
"Raise your words, not your voice."

For in the stillness, truth abounds,
Where whispers carry profound sounds,
With eloquence, we can empower,
And let our inner voice shower.

It is rain that nurtures, that feeds,
Not the thunder's destructive deeds,
Through gentle drops, empathy shows,
And understanding freely flows.

So let your words bloom like a flower,
With kindness, they hold mighty power,
In every conversation's hour,
Let love and compassion devour.

Spreading like petals, soft and light,
Bringing a sense of peace at night,
For it is the gentle breeze that's heard,
Not the storm's destructive word.

Embrace the calm, let anger cease,
Let voices echo with inner peace,
For unity to reign and ignite,
A symphony sung in words that delight.

So remember, when storms try to rule,
And chaos threatens to overrule,
Let kindness and grace be your choice,
Raise your words, not your voice.

For in the rain's touch, the flowers grow,
And with gentle words, compassion will flow,
In this symphony, let us all rejoice,
Raise your words, not your voice.

Real Queens Fix Each Other's Crown

In a kingdom of strength and grace profound,
Where real queens with love and kindness abound,
They understand the power that lies within,
To uplift each other through thick and thin.

They know that life's trials can leave hearts aching,
And doubts and worries can be overtaking,
But these true queens remain steadfast and true,
Supporting and fixing each other's crown anew.

With gentle hands and words, they tend to heal,
Knowing that unity is what they must reveal,
They brush away sorrows with empathy deep,
Guiding one another through challenges they keep.

Together they weave a tapestry of trust,
Building each other up, never causing a fuss,
For in the sisterhood, they find the strength,
To conquer any obstacle, no matter the length.

They share in triumphs and celebrate with pride,
For real queens empower and stand by each other's side,
In unity and confidence, they truly shine,
Knowing their worth, their worth is divine.

No rivalry or envy can break their sacred bond,
For real queens know selfishness is beyond,
Instead, they embrace their unique majesty,
And recognize the beauty in others they see.

So let us learn from these queens so grand,
To lend a helping hand, always understand,
That fixing each other's crowns is a noble art,
For real queens bring light and love to every part.

She Isn't Fragile Like A Flower.
She Is Fragile Like A Bomb.

Oh, she walks with grace, her beauty unfurled,
A delicate petal, yet a heart of coal.
Her smile can light up the darkest night,
But beneath it lies a power so bright.

She isn't fragile like a flower that bends,
No, she's fragile like a bomb that descends.
One wrong move, one misplaced word,
Can cause an explosion, a shattered world.

Her touch ignites a fire so true,
It melts the ice; it burns through you.
She wears her strength like a crown of thorns,
A fragility that can tear the dawn.

So tread with care, oh mortal man,
For in her eyes, a storm brews can.
She isn't fragile like a flower that fades,
No, she's fragile like a bomb that waits.

She Needed A Hero, So That's What She Became

In a world where darkness tried to claim,
She needed a hero, so that's what she became.
With fiery passion, she faced the night,
A valiant warrior embracing the fight.

No longer a damsel in distress,
She shattered chains and surpassed duress.
Summoning courage from deep within,
She let her spirit rise and begin.

Through battles fought and battles won,
She proved to all she was second to none.
Using strength and wisdom to guide her way,
She forged her fate, flaws on full display.

A bonfire of hope, a light so bright,
She defied odds with all her might.
Inspiring others with her fearless soul,
Unyielding, determined to reach her goal.

With each trial and tribulation she faced,
She carved her destiny with unwavering grace.
Unafraid of the demons that taunted her mind,
She embraced challenges, leaving them all behind.

From the ashes of her past she arose,
A courageous spirit only she knows.
To be her own hero was no easy feat,
But she embraced the challenge, never accepting defeat.

She taught us all a valuable lesson,
That through adversity we can find our confession.
To rise above, to prevail in our own right,
To become our own heroes and shine with might.

For within each of us lies the flame,
To conquer the darkness, to stake our claim.
She needed a hero, so that's what she became,
A symbol of strength, a warrior's name.

She Never Cared For A Crown. She Preferred A Sword

In a realm where legends thrive and tales are told,
There stood a spirit resolute and bold.
A woman of prowess, a warrior pure,
She never cared for a crown; she preferred a sword.

With blades as her voice, and armour as her skin,
She conquered the battles; her heart did win.
The elegant grace of a queen, she held,
But her true majesty was in the sword she wield.

No jewels could match the gleam of her blade,
For honour and justice, she valiantly swayed.
She eschewed the trappings that burdened the crown,
Opting for freedom in battle's renown.

In every skirmish, she fought with might,
Unyielding, unfaltering, her warrior's right.
Her spirit aflame with unwavering zeal,
She epitomized strength, her heart a steel.

Though thrones may entice with their opulent glow,
She chose the sword's path, the adventured show.
For in the clashing of swords and battle's engross,
She found her true purpose and fulfilled her ethos.

A crown may shine, but it's a fleeting delight,
While the sword endures, in valour's pure light.
With every strike and parry, she displayed,
The power within, on the sword's path she stayed.

So let her be known as the swordsmith's ward,
A woman of might who wielded her sword.
She never cared for a crown, it needs be explored,
For her heart belonged to the battles she scored.

She Remembered Who She Was, And The Game Changed

In a world of chaos and shifting tides,
Amidst the storms that raged and skies that cried,
A soul, once lost, sought to find her way,
To remember who she was, come what may.

She treaded with courage, in darkness she roamed,
Seeking the truth, she refused to be disowned,
For deep within her, a fire burned bright,
Guiding her path with its eternal light.

Through battlefields of doubt and fear,
She forged ahead, her purpose clear,
No longer a pawn in life's wicked game,
She owned her existence, and claimed her name.

With every setback, she found her strength,
Resilient and fierce, beyond all lengths,
The game changed its tune, as she took control,
Unleashing her power, body and soul.

She remembered the magic that lay within,
A force so potent, no barrier could win,
She danced in freedom, unshackled and free,
Embracing her essence, living authentically.

No longer defined by society's mold,
She embraced her worth, a story untold,
A phoenix arose from the ashes of her past,
Boundless and majestic, a legacy to last.

With each breath she took, the universe sighed,
For in her existence, it was glorified,
She remembered who she was, and the game changed,
A victor emerged, no longer estranged.

She Used To Be The Sweetest Girl...

Once upon a time, in a world so bright,
She was the sweetest girl, a radiant light.
Gentle smile, heart pure as pearls unfurled,
Innocence danced in the curls that curled.

That was me, once upon a distant day,
Basking in kindness, in love's warm array.
Words like honey, actions soft and kind,
In a garden of grace, I used to find.

Time has passed, seasons come and gone,
Yet memories linger, like an eternal dawn.
The sweetest girl, a faded memory's swirl,
Whispers softly, "That was me... I was the sweetest girl."

She Wore Her Scars As Her Best Attire, A Stunning Dress Made Of Hellfire.

*She wore her scars as her best attire,
A stunning dress made of hellfire.
Each mark told a story, etched on her skin,
The battles fought, the pain within.*

*Her shoulders adorned with battle's embrace,
Searing marks that time couldn't erase.
From nights of torment to mornings fought,
Her scars, a testament of battles she sought.*

*In her eyes, there gleamed a fiery passion,
Burning fiercely, defying all ration.
For she had learned, through piercing pain,
That strength arises from ashes and flame.*

*Her soul ablaze, with resilience ablare,
She let her scars dance, unashamedly bare.
With every step, she radiated might,
Her scars, badges of honour shining bright.*

*No longer ashamed, she embraced her past,
For it made her strong, a survivor steadfast.
She wore her scars, a symbol of power,
A warrior's spirit, blooming like a flower.*

People whispered, awe in their voice,
As they witnessed her grace, stunning and choice.
For she proved beauty isn't just skin deep,
It resides in hearts, where true warriors sleep.

Some People Survive Chaos, And That Is How They Grow,
I Thrive In Chaos Because That Is All I Know.

In a world of turmoil and strife,
Where chaos reigns and order's life,
Some folks may cower and hide,
But I, I thrive in this tide.

The stormy seas of change I've braved,
And weathered every raging wave,
For in the eye of the hurricane,
I've found a strange and fierce serenity to crave.

The wreckage of the past I've surveyed,
And from the ruins, I've built my day,
For in the ashes of what's lost,
I've found the strength to rise and boast.

The chaos of the world may rage,
But in my heart, I've found a cage,
A sanctuary of hope and might,
Where I can face the darkness of the night.

So let the winds of change blow strong,
And let the thunder of the storm all day long,
For in the eye of the hurricane,
I'll find my strength and keep on sway.

Sometimes, Happy Memories Hurt The Most

Sometimes, happy memories hurt the most,
Like gentle thorns that prick the heart's repose.
For in their sweetness lies a lingering ghost,
A bittersweet reminder of what was once close.

Their whispers echo through the corridors of time,
Tugging at the strings of emotions intertwined.
The laughter and joy now stained with a rhyme,
Leaving an ache, a longing that's hard to define.

Those cherished moments, etched upon the soul,
Now bring tears that silently roll.
The smiles we shared, no longer whole,
They haunt us, pierce us, taking their toll.

Yet still, we hold on to those fragments of bliss,
Clutching tightly to the memories we miss.
For even though they cause our hearts to twist,
They remind us of a love we'd never dismiss.

Speak The Truth, Even If Your Voice Shakes

When shadows lengthen, doubts take flight,
Speak the truth with all your might.
Though fear may tremble in your voice,
Let honesty be your steadfast choice.

In moments when the world seems dark,
Let truth shine bright, a guiding spark.
Through turmoil's storm and falsehood's quake,
Stand firm, speak true for honour's sake.

Brave the tempest, face the fear,
Let integrity ring loud and clear.
For in the echo of your words,
Resides the strength that truth affords.

So let your voice shake in its might,
A beacon in the darkest night.
For in the end, it's not the calm,
But honest truth that brings us balm.

Sun-Moon

Everyone becomes my sun,
When I need a guiding flower.
But what about when I needed a moon,
Guiding me in my darkest hour?

When darkness descended like a shroud,
And shadows loomed, my heart was loud,
I needed a light to guide my way,
A beacon to chase the night away.

But you, my friends, became my sun,
Warming my soul with love so won,
Your smiles and laughter lit the night,
And filled my heart with delight.

As flowers bloomed, our bond did too,
In gardens of love, we grew,
Together we danced, under the stars,
Our hearts entwined, like twinkling Mars.

But then, the darkness had its say,
And tried to snuff out the light of day,
It whispered lies, and sowed despair,
And made me doubt, and filled me with fear.

Everyone becomes my sun,
When I need a guiding flower.
But what about when I needed a moon,
Guiding me in my darkest hour?

The Beautiful Spring Came, And When Nature Resumes Her Loveliness, The Human Soul Is Apt To Revive Also.

In the heart of spring's sweet embrace we find,
Nature's beauty, in full bloom, enshrined.
As blossoms burst forth with vibrant glee,
The human soul too finds solace and glee.

Renewed by the earth's awakening grace,
Our spirits lifted in this wondrous place.
A dance of life in colours arrayed,
Hope and joy in every cascade.

With each bloom, a whisper of rebirth,
Awakening dreams long held in dearth.
Nature's cycle, a gentle reminder,
That within us all, there's room to kindle.

So let us revel in this season's call,
Embrace the beauty that surrounds us all.
For when spring paints its canvas anew,
Our souls revive, refreshed and true

The Darkest Nights Produce The Brightest Stars

In the darkest nights when shadows embrace,
There lies a truth, a celestial grace,
From depths of despair, hope still finds its way,
The brightest stars emerge, casting doubts away.

Through trials and tribulations we tread,
A journey where dreams may seem all but dead,
But hold your gaze up to the midnight sky,
For there, constellations dance, never shy.

Each flickering light, a tale of fight,
Of souls who refused to surrender their might,
They shimmer and glow with resilience profound,
Guiding lost hearts, where hope can be found.

Though darkness looms, it cannot dim their glow,
Those radiant stars, they never refuse to bow low,
They whisper, "Do not fear the night,
For within its grasp, lies infinite light."

The Language Of Dance

In silence speaks the dance's tongue,
Fluid motions, a tale unsung.
A choreography of hearts aflame,
Expressed in steps without a name.

Through pirouettes and graceful spins,
Emotions rise, where words begin.
A language pure, devoid of sound,
In every leap, a story found.

With each movement, a narrative unfolds,
Of joy, of sorrow, untold.
The language of dance, a symphony bright,
Painting feelings in the darkest night.

In leaps and bounds, the soul takes flight,
Transcending barriers, reaching heights.
Body whispers secrets deep,
In the language of dance, we truly speak.

The Power of Imagination Makes Us Infinite

In realms where boundless dreams take flight,
Imagination weaves its light,
A tapestry of endless might,
Expanding our internal height.

Through thoughts that soar and minds unchained,
New worlds and wonders are ordained,
Infinite vistas, unrestrained,
Within our minds, true freedom gained.

No limits here, no walls to bind,
Invention's spark ignites the mind,
With visions bold, our spirits find
That in imagination, we're aligned.

So let us dream and boldly create,
For in this realm, there is no fate,
The power of imagination, great,
Makes us infinite, at any rate.

The Scariest Moment Is Always Before You Start

In shadows deep, where fears reside,
The scariest moment, amplified,
Looms large before your eager heart,
Just as you prepare to start.

Unknown paths, veiled in doubt,
Whispers of anxiety shout,
Yet within that daunting space,
Resides the promise of embrace.

Courage whispers, softly clear,
Breaking through the fog of fear,
For in the realm of the unknown,
Seeds of growth are wildly sown.

Embrace the tremble, take the leap,
From the edge, your soul shall steep,
The scariest moment slowly departs,
As courage blooms within your heart.

The Scariest Monsters Are The Ones That Lurk Within Our Souls

In shadows deep, where darkness dwells,
The scariest monsters, their stories tell,
Not under beds or in the night,
But within our souls, out of sight.

They whisper doubts, they breed despair,
Feeding on our deepest fears with care,
Cloaked in masks of our own making,
These inner demons, ever waking.

They thrive on chaos, on inner strife,
Haunting every corner of our life,
Yet courage shines a guiding light,
To battle these beasts, to face the fight.

The Sound Of Joy

In whispers of wind and laughter's sweet chime,
Joy serenades the heart, transcending time.
It echoes in a child's carefree song,
In melodies of belonging, pure and strong.

A symphony of love, each note sincere,
Resonates through moments held dear.
Birdsong at dawn, a tranquil stream's flow,
Whispers of joy wherever we go.

Laughter bubbling like a brook's playful glee,
Echoes of happiness dancing free.
Joy sounds like a sunrise, golden and bright,
A chorus of gladness in day and night.

It sings in embraces, in friendships that bind,
In shared laughter, true connections we find.
Joy's sound, a harmony of souls aligned,
A timeless melody, forever entwined.

The Truth Is... I Am Not Sorry...
Why Should I Be Sorry For The Things You Did?

The truth is bold, it stands its ground,
Unwavering in the face of sound.
I am not sorry for what you've done,
Why should I pay for battles won?

You took your path, made your choice,
Now hear my unwavering voice.
Apologies linger not in my heart,
For I won't play a false part.

Your deeds, your words, they define you,
In this world, actions ring true.
I won't bear the weight of your sin,
For my spirit soars from within.

Let regrets wither, let them fade,
In truth's light, no masquerade.
I stand tall, unburdened and free,
No apology will you hear from me.

The Truth? We'll Never Have Today Again.

In fleeting time we find our truth,
Today, a gift, a precious youth.
Moments slip like grains of sand,
Hold them close within your hand.

The past is gone, tomorrow unknown,
Embrace today, let seeds be sown.
For what we have is here and now,
A chance to live, to learn, to vow.

Each sunrise brings a brand new start,
A canvas waiting for your art.
So seize the day with all your might,
Make every moment pure and bright.

For time's swift arrow will not stall,
The present fades, like echoes fall.
Live today as if your last breath nears,
Cherish each second, conquer fears.

Let laughter ring, let love abound,
In every heartbeat, joy resound.
For the truth that we will never regain,
Is today, this moment we attain.

The Woods Are Lovely, Dark, And Deep, But I Have Promises To Keep, And Miles To Go Before I Sleep

In woods of whispers, secrets keep,
Where shadows dance and dreams do sweep.
A world of darkness, beauty steep,
But promises beckon from slumber's leap.

Miles untraveled, a journey long,
Before I rest where stars belong.
Through winding paths, my spirit throngs,
In the hush of night, I find my song.

Whispers of leaves and moonlit glow,
Guide me forward, through ebb and flow.
Each step a vow, each breath a show,
To keep my word, to let life grow.

So in this wood, so dark, so deep,
I'll venture forth, my promises to keep.
With miles ahead, through fate's grand sweep,
I embrace the night, before I sleep.

The Word "Father" Rotted In My Mouth

In silence, shadows of memory's shroud,
The word "Father" rotted in my mouth,
A bitter taste, a solemn vow avowed,
Echoes of absence, grief's enduring drouth.

Each syllable tainted, laden with pain,
Whispers of love lost in sorrow's embrace,
Memories like petals in autumn rain,
Fading echoes of a familiar grace.

The void he left, a cavern vast and deep,
An ache that lingers, a wound untold,
In the silence where his whispers sleep,
A poignant tale of love now cold.

Yet within this decay, a seed takes root,
A legacy cherished, a bond unbroken,
In the heart's hallowed chamber, resolute,
Where the word "Father" is softly spoken.

The Wound Is The Place Where The Light Enters You

In the darkness of a soul's deep night,
Where shadows dance and fears take flight,
There lies a wound, raw and true,
A portal for the light to pierce through.

Through cracks in our broken facade,
Shines the brilliance of the divine rod,
Each fracture a pathway for grace,
To mend our spirits, to embrace.

Embrace the hurt, the ache, the pain,
For there, new beginnings gain.
The light enters where we're torn,
To heal, to mend, to be reborn.

So welcome the light, let it ignite,
The wounded parts that ache in spite,
For from the depths, new strength accrues,
The wound, a place where light imbues.

There Is Always A Way Out For Those Clever Enough To Find It

~Percy Jackson: The Titan's Curse
In twists and turns, life may entwine,
A labyrinth of challenges divine.
But fear not, dear heart, for there's a way out,
If you're clever, you'll find no doubt.

Through every obstacle, keep your wits keen,
And search for the hidden glean.
With persistence and grace, you'll unseen,
A path that will lead you to serene.

Though darkness may seem to abound,
And shadows cast doubts profound,
Hold fast to hope, let it resound,
For in the end, a solution will astound.

So take heart, dear one, and don't despair,
For there's always a way out, beyond compare.
Keep searching, keep striving, and never fare,
For with wit and will, you'll emerge from the snare.

There Is Nothing Either Good, Or Bad, But The Thinking Makes It So

In realms of thought, perceptions sway,
What's good or bad, in mind does play.
Through shifting lens of our belief,
Reality finds no sure relief.

For what we hold within our mind,
Defines the hue by which we find,
The world around us, shaped anew,
By thoughts we cherish, deemed as true.

A rose may bloom, a thorn may sting,
Yet in our minds, their meanings ring.
It's not the object, pure and sure,
But thoughts we weave, emotions pure.

So let us ponder, deep and clear,
That good and bad are not so near,
Inherent in an act or show,
But in the minds where meanings grow.

They Broke The Wrong Parts Of Me.
They Broke My Wings And Forgot I Had Claws.

In shimmering shards of shadows, I once soared on wings so free,
A celestial creature of wonder, a dream of grace and glee.
But they broke the wrong parts of me, they shattered my wings so bright,
And left me crippled and alone, with only tears to fight.

They forgot that I had claws, sharp talons of might,
That could tear through the darkness, and rend the night.
But they broke my wings, and left me to fall,
A fragile, helpless thing, a shadow of my wall.

Oh, how they broke the wrong parts of me,
And left me to bleed and be.
But still I hold on to my claws,
And dream of soaring once more, in the skies of pause.

For though they broke my wings, they could not break my heart,
For in the shards of shadows, I am still a work of art.
And though I cannot fly, I will not be tamed,
For I am a creature of wonder, with claws unnamed.

They Asked- Don't You Feel Lonely Living In Your Own World?
I Whispered- Don't You Feel Powerless Living In Other People's Worlds?

In my own world, I find solace and peace
A place where I can be me, without cease
I dance to the beat of my own drum
And let my imagination take flight, like a hummingbird

But in others' worlds, I often feel confined
A stranger in a land that is not mine
I long to break free from their chains
And soar high above, like a bird in spring rains

They ask me if I don't feel lonely here
Living in this world that's far from clear
But I reply, "Don't you feel powerless there?"
Trapped in a life that's not truly fair

For in their worlds, I am but a guest
A fleeting presence, at best
I yearn for a home where I can rest
Where my soul can sing, and my heart can nest

So I hold on to my dreams and desires
And keep dancing, through all the fires
For one day, I'll find my true abode
Where I can live and love, as I have always known.

They're Villains...But Why?

In a world of tales spun with ink,
Where villains linger, dark and distinct,
Their deeds condemned, their souls confined,
But the question remains, why behind?

We were told their hearts held shadows deep,
Stained by actions that made angels weep.
Yet no one dared to seek the truth,
To understand the reasons uncouth.

What led them astray, down wicked paths?
Were they born twisted, like nature's wrath?
Or did life's tempests mold their hearts,
Shaping villains from innocent starts?

Perhaps it was pain, a bitter sting,
That turned their hopes to an evil thing.
Neglected love, a broken trust,
Kindling fury, in ashes thrust.

Some may have danced with desperation's tune,
Caught in webs that society spun too soon.
Echoes of injustice silenced their plea,
Forcing rebellion, their only decree.

Or were they victims of circumstance,
Haunted by choices they couldn't enhance?
Bound by circumstances beyond control,
Their moral compass lost, a rudderless soul.

Let us not forget, in our righteous stride,
To question the motives, delve deeper inside.
For villains are not mere shades of black,
But stories untold, taking a different track.

Thunderstorms

In the realm of thunder's might,
Nature's fury takes its flight.
With roaring clouds and lightning's gleam,
A tempest's dance, a thunderous dream.

"Why do you like such storms?" they ask,
A fiery tempest, nature's task.
I simply smile, my reasons clear,
For storms possess an essence dear.

It shows that even nature knows,
The need to scream as passion flows.
With rumbling thunder, echoes loud,
A symphony, a voice unbound.

Within the chaos, skies collide,
A power felt deep in one's pride.
A reminder fierce, yet so sublime,
That even heavens yearn to chime.

The rain cascades as tears descend,
And hidden fears, the storm may mend.
For through the tempest's raging wail,
Nature too finds solace in the gale.

With each flash and booming roll,
The storm's release, a sacred stole.
It tells a tale of strength untamed,
A beauty fierce, never to be named.

In every crackle, every boom,
A burst of life within the gloom.
Nature wears its heart upon its sleeve,
Through thunder's chant, it seeks reprieve.

So, to the storm, I raise my praise,
For all its wild and rhythmic craze.
A vivid display of nature's might,
A reminder true, of life's own fight.

For storms, they show both grace and ire,
A rebirth for a soul on fire.
So, why do I love thunder's chime?
Because even nature needs to scream sometimes.

To Be A Star, You Must Burn

To be a star, you must burn bright,
A fire within, a dazzling light.
Through trials fierce, you'll find your way,
In darkest night, you'll still convey.

Each challenge met with fervent flame,
Embracing heat, you rise the same.
To shine so high, you pay the cost,
In glowing embers, dreams embossed.

From ashes born, a spirit new,
Resilience shaped, in skies of blue.
So heed this call, oh soul so yearn,
To be a star, you must burn.

***To Live Is The Rarest Thing In The World.
Most People Exist, That Is All***

*Life's a wild ride, don't you see,
To truly live, that's the key.
Most just drift, day by day,
Existence dull, in a monotonous way.*

*Adventure calls, dreams to chase,
Don't settle for a humdrum pace.
Embrace each moment, big or small,
Living fully, standing tall.*

*So break free from the ordinary grind,
Let passion and purpose intertwine.
Don't just exist, but truly thrive,
For to live is the rarest thing alive.*

We Are All Born So Beautiful, The Greatest Tragedy Is Being Convinced We Are Not

In every soul, a beauty born so bright,
A spark of light that shines with pure delight.
Yet shadows creep, convincing hearts to mourn,
The greatest tragedy: ourselves forlorn.

From tender start, we glow with inner grace,
Each face a masterpiece, a unique trace.
But whispers cruel, they weave a tangled plot,
Convincing us we're lacking, beauty forgot.

Oh, tragic tale of minds misled astray,
By doubts that steal our radiance away.
Embrace the truth, within you lies the key,
To see the beauty, set your spirit free.

For we are born resplendent, shining true,
A masterpiece in every point of view.
Reject the lie that tells you otherwise,
And let your beauty soar, beyond the skies.

We Cannot Become What We Want By Remaining What We Are

Embrace the winds of change, don't fear to part,
For growth demands a shift, a brand new start.
In stagnant waters, dreams fade out of sight,
To reach new heights, shed old skin in the light.

Comfort's embrace can lull ambitions to sleep,
But daring souls their destinies will reap.
To soar among the stars, we must first change,
Break free from shadows, into the unknown range.

The caterpillar knows to become the butterfly,
Its form must alter, its spirit must defy.
So too must we shed our former self's guise,
To grasp the future, where our true self lies.

Stand not in place, afraid to take that leap,
The path to greatness is not for the meek.
For we cannot be what we truly aspire,
Without shedding skins of old, higher we'll aspire.

What Lies Behind Us And What Lies Before Us Are Tiny Matters Compared To What Lies Within Us

What lies behind, a fading past,
Memories held, they never last.
What lies ahead, the unknown lands,
Tomorrow's dreams in shifting sands.

But what within, a boundless sea,
Depth of soul, vast mystery.
Courage, love, and strength untold,
Treasures hidden, waiting to unfold.

In every heart, a universe whole,
Infinite potential, a timeless scroll.
What lies within, a guiding light,
Illuminating the darkest night.

So fear not what the future brings,
Nor dwell on long-forgotten things.
For what lies deep inside each of us,
Is where true power and beauty discuss.

What's A Queen Without Her King?
Well, Historically Speaking, More Powerful

In fair kingdoms of yore, a tale to be told,
Of queens and their kings, with wisdom untold.
For though love may bind them, with a powerful sway,
Historically speaking, the queen held more in a way.

A queen, so regal, her presence supreme,
With strength and conviction, her power would gleam.
She stood by her king, with grace unsurpassed,
Yet behind the scenes, her influence would amass.

In battles of thrones, and political might,
The queen held the cards, and played them just right.
A strategist shrewd, in the game of the realm,
She navigated wars, with a steady helm.

While the king, bold and brave, commanded the troops,
The queen, wise and astute, controlled the group.
She advised with insight, her wisdom revealed,
Her counsel, a treasure, the king would wield.

With diplomacy firm, she built alliances strong,
Manipulating the threads, weaving peace all along.
While the king fought on fields, with a sword in his hand,
The queen fought behind, orchestrating the land.

Her intelligence vast, her wit razor-sharp,
The queen ruled with vigour, leaving no mark.
A ruler in her own right, with power unseen,
Historically speaking, the queen reigned supreme.

So let us remember, in tales long gone by,
The queens who, behind thrones, made kingdoms fly.
Though hidden from sight, their influence so grand,
In the annals of history, they'll forever stand.

When You Get Tired, Learn To Rest, Not To Quit

When weariness weighs upon your soul,
And life's burdens take their toll,
Learn to rest, not to quit the race,
Find solace in a tranquil space.

Rest, like a whispering breeze at dawn,
Rejuvenates the spirit withdrawn,
Gathers strength for the onward climb,
Renews the hope, lost in time.

In moments when the journey feels long,
When shadows dance and doubts throng,
Pause, breathe deep, let serenity knit
A respite to refresh, not to forfeit.

For in the stillness of repose,
New vigour within you grows,
Embrace the quiet, the gentle respite,
Forge ahead with revived delight.

So when tiredness calls your name,
Remember, rest is not a shame,
It's a pause, a momentary transit,
To uplift your weary spirit.

Who Needs A Prince When You're Already A Queen?

In a world of dreams and make-believe scenes,
Who needs a prince when you're already a queen?
A crown of confidence, a heart that gleams,
You reign over challenges with graceful sheen.

No castle walls can confine your soul's flight,
With wisdom as your sceptre, shining bright.
Through trials and triumphs, you stand upright,
A ruler of your destiny, day and night.

So wear your crown, let your spirit be seen,
For in your essence, true power convenes.
Embrace your throne, where strength convenes,
Who needs a prince when you're already a queen?

You Don't Understand. It's Not That I Can't Love.
It's That I'm Afraid Of It.

In shadows deep, my heart does hide,
A place where fears and doubts abide.
You don't understand, you cannot see,
The walls I've built so carefully.

It's not that I can't love, you know,
But seeds of doubt within me sow.
Afraid of love, its power strong,
To break me down, where I belong.

The vulnerability it demands,
Terrifies me, where I stand.
I long for love, yet pull away,
Scared of the price that I might pay.

You Have To Be Odd To Be Number One

In a world where normal reigns supreme,
To stand out, you must dare to dream.
For greatness lies in the unconventional way,
Embrace your oddity, let it lead the way.

You have to be odd to be number one,
A solitary star against the setting sun.
Unique and quirky, a different beat,
In a crowd of followers, be the one who's fleet.

Embrace your quirks, let them shine bright,
In a sea of conformity, be the guiding light.
For it's the oddities that make us unique,
The unconventional path, the bold critique.

So march to your own drum, don't shy away,
Be odd, be different, let your colours display.
For in a world of norms and rules set,
It's the odd ones who truly place their bet.

You Know What The Weirdest Is For Me?
I Don't Cry When I Lose The People I Love
Anymore...

In depths of sorrow veiled, a heart compelled,
A strange lament, a truth that cuts so deep.
For once a tear cascaded, freely welled,
But now, a barren soul, no tears to weep.

What strangeness this, a path of hardened clay,
Where love's departure leaves no trace of rain.
Gone are the tears that once could gently sway,
Now lost souls slip away without the pain.

Oh, what a curious fate has befallen,
To lose so many, yet no tears descend.
A stoic stance, a heart that's now swollen,
With grief unspoken, wounds that never mend.

But does this mean love's essence has grown thin?
Or is it strength that keeps the tears within?

Though tears may not fall, love still lingers deep,
In every cherished memory we hold.
For loss may leave a void, a soul to keep,
Yet love's eternal flame cannot be cold.

The heart, a vessel strong, resilient, true,
Where love's sweet essence dwells, forever pure.
Though tears may not caress the cheeks anew,
Their absence does not love's embrace obscure.

For in the stillness of a tearless night,
A silent prayer, a whisper to the sky,
Each lost soul, bathed in love's eternal light,
Shall find solace, as tears softly pass by.

You Must Forge Your Own Path For It To Mean Anything

~The Heroes of Olympus: The Lost Hero

In life, you hold the pen that writes your fate,
Each line and verse, a choice, a weight.
To find your meaning, don't follow the crowd,
For true purpose is found in what you allow.

Do not let others dictate where you go,
Embrace your dreams, though they may seem slow.
The journey of self-discovery takes time,
But the reward is worth every moment divine.

Seek out new experiences, explore and dare,
Don't be afraid to stumble or show care.
Learn from each step, each misstep too,
And know that growth comes from all you do.

Forge your own path, let your heart lead,
And though the road may twist and turn, heed.
Your unique voice will ring loud and clear,
When you embrace the journey without fear.

So take up the challenge, seize the day,
And make your mark upon the world in play.
For when you forge your own path, you'll see,
A life filled with purpose, wild and free.

www.ingramcontent.com/pod-product-compliance
Lightning Source LLC
LaVergne TN
LVHW041951070526
838199LV00051BA/2987